AUDACITY TO SPEAK

Finding the Power to Be Your Most Authentic Self

ANEESHA JACKO

Copyright © 2022 Aneesha Jacko

All Rights Reserved.

ISBN: 979-8-9-87167908

First Edition

The contents of this book may not be reproduced, duplicated, or transmitted in any form, or by any means, electronic, photocopying, mechanical, recording, or otherwise, without direct, prior written permission of the author.

Disclaimer: All attempts have been made by the author to provide factual and accurate content. Information and advice in this book are to be followed at the discretion of the reader.

DEDICATION

This book is dedicated with love to my boys Sy and Avi. May you always use your voice in a powerful way. #31 Love you forever!

What They're Saying About *Audacity to Speak*

Audacity to Speak means being unapologetic about articulating your point of view regardless of how it makes people feel. Fearlessly, what Jacko has taught me is how to express myself in a nice way without affecting people which has brought me a community and I thank her for that. I am proud of her for having the Audacity to Speak herself.

— **Dame Dash, Author of** *Culture Vulture*

Audacity to Speak is inspiring, insightful, and influential to those who are ready to speak up, stand out and make meaningful connections. Aneesha Jacko shows that by finding the courage to unmute herself, her world and the world around her began to come together in the most impactful way. If you're ready to show up and be seen, heard and build everlasting relationships this book is for you.

— **Dr. Jill Kahn, Author of** *The Gift of Taking, Honor Yourself First… All Else Will Follow*

Audacity to Speak is such a gift to anyone who is finally mastering the courage to use their voice and share their gifts or talents with the world. Aneesha has been such a courageous leader modeling the importance of finding and using her voice, in an inspiring and intentional way. A MUST read for all future leaders of the world.

— **Brianna Greenspan, Author of** *The Miracle Morning Art of Affirmations*

CONTENTS

Chapter 1:

I Can't Hear You: The Power of Unmuting 1

Chapter 2:

Transactional or Transformational 17

Chapter 3:

Conversational Intelligence. 23

Chapter 4:

Examining Talk and Trust 29

Chapter 5:

Take the Day On 43

Chapter 6:

The Results are In 57

Chapter 7:

Conclusion 67

Appendix 73

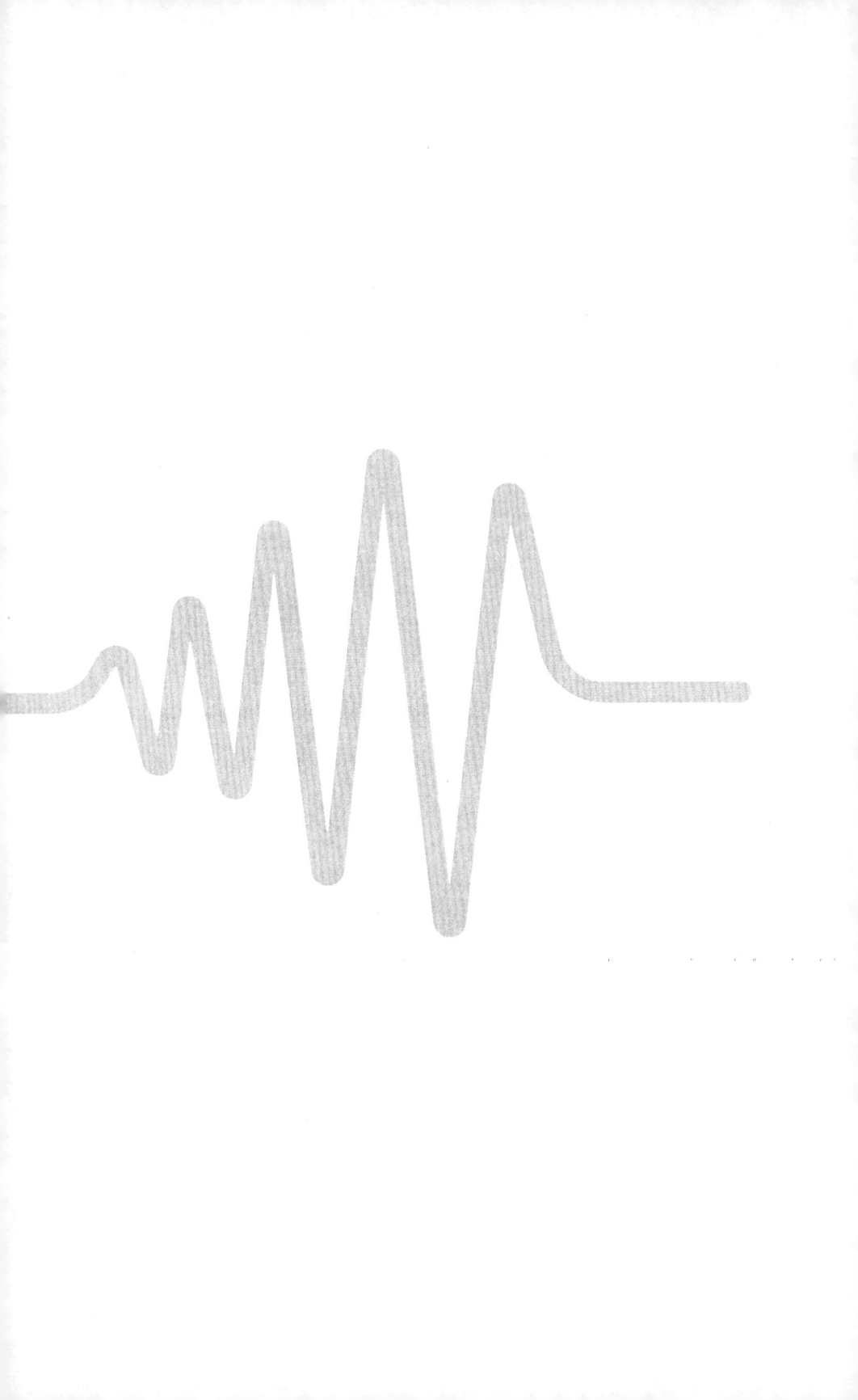

— CHAPTER 1 —

I Can't Hear You: The Power of Unmuting

*T*hink about the sound of your own voice. What do you hear? What is important or valuable to you? What makes you uniquely you? Your voice is your most powerful asset. Yet, too many of us shy away from using it, or we may even silence ourselves for fear of what others may think or how they may perceive us. As a result, we often don't say what needs to be said when it needs to be said. We minimize our power and lessen our impact.

In this book, I want to challenge you to unlearn the power of silence; instead, we all must embrace the *Audacity to Speak*.

Audacity to Speak inspired me to break out of my comfort zone in order to be my true authentic self. Pastor Colon felt privileged to be asked to be in our company of leaders from around the world led by Dr. Dennis McKesey, CEO of Off School Grounds, Inc. Pastor Colon shared that audacity and courage equal the ability to move minds. We as leaders are doing amazing work by standing in the gap for those who are powerless and are not able to make an impact.

My Calling

Specifically, one day, during a prayer, Pastor Colon spoke and said: "The prophetic utterance of an Aneesha." Upon hearing these words, I froze. I couldn't believe that someone who never met me spoke into my life in such a powerful way. "Of these things, we rejoice in the success." These are the things that propel John; everything hinges on leadership. A movement is more than a moment. Every choice that we make now will impact our future. We march today to communicate our feelings about our current state of affairs. We all watched George Floyd with deep sorrow, but when I heard him call out "mama", there was something different about the cadence of his voice that was felt in the heart of anyone who ever cared for a child. We know the cry for help when our children call us. While in the middle of a pandemic, where things were uncertain and everything was shut down, we all had to STOP. But his cry for his mother got our attention and action followed. Pastor Colon shared that we should not be ashamed of our plight. We have agency as leaders and a right to engage and fight to speak. We should always expect excellence. Knowing who you are changes the actuality of what is going on and what will be. Make a reference to show them who you are. Awareness didn't change the chokehold, but the moment he decided to remember and say it everything changed. Being aware of who we are can break strongholds and change the direction of our life. As I listened to these powerful words and thought about their implications, a seed for writing this book was planted.

As I think about the catalyst for writing this book, I thank God for challenges. I have higher heights to go to in life. Pastor Colon declared and decreed that I would get what I want and that the power of life and death was in our tongue. He shared that we should put our hands on what we want to prosper, demand that it can succeed, and go after it. Furthermore, he reminded me that God is bigger than any situation that either you or I will face. In other words, our ability to overcome is etched on our DNA.

As these words were shared, I remember clearly speaking to Dame Dash and Dennis over two weeks before and being asked what I dreamt about. I was stuck, and for the first time speechless. Dame asked me what I wanted next, and I was on mute. I had no words to express my hopes and dreams about my future. He pointed out that not only was I being selfish, but I was not setting the right example for my own children. As a wife, mom, and leader, I have to constantly be an example. Now, in this case, I had to take a self-inventory, and I came up short. My story begins with the feeling that it is finally time to take action and to create a legacy that will benefit not just my children but my children's children. But I did not stop there. I used this as an opportunity to pivot. Dennis shared in a meeting how important creating opportunities off school grounds to lead and serve in communities throughout the world is so necessary, so I began to dream and to wonder.

Evaluating my past, I also realized the trauma and disappointments that I have had. I understand that by shifting my perspective I now know that I am bigger than my past, and my future is greater than my faults or shortcomings. It is my job to break generational strongholds of feeling inadequate and complacent. It is time to move in a new direction.

The Muted Scholar

I was a happy child. As a young scholar I loved school, and I maintained good grades. Success was important to me, but my understanding of what success looked like with me changed when I was in the first grade. One day I was sitting in class and there was a storm, and it was dark outside. Suddenly lightning flashed by our window, and one of my classmates screamed. I, of course, was scared, but I stayed still. The teacher singled me out, yelled at me, and told me to go sit in the corner. I was devastated. I couldn't believe that she would separate me from the whole class. I think it is important to share that I was the only girl of color in the class of thirty-two. The trauma of being in spaces that are not racially accepting while also being treated unkindly hurt and cause my decline around my ability to thrive in school. Although I remained in the top classes, I was always spoken to with a voice of criticism and lack of love. I felt invisible in school. At that moment I shut my voice off. I was afraid to speak up for myself. I was muted.

Imagine being in spaces and places that don't cultivate young scholars, where yelling and shouting is acceptable. It traumatized me and made me feel lost at school. I was unaware of the joy that could be found in school. I already saw myself differently whether it was from the location of my school community, the texture of my hair, the color of my skin or who picked me up from school. It all matters. We have to understand how important the formative years of school are for children. We learn to use our gifts and talents in meaningful ways, connecting to new experiences every day. Learning to speak has to be aligned to state goals with an understanding of the emotional needs of a child for their present and their future. A quote from Bobby Kountz that resonates with me is that "Gratitude is the capacity to retrieve childhood genius at will." I am grateful for every experience that I have had to be where I am today.

Legacy Starts Now

Legacy now is about sharing what you have learned, not just bequeathing valuables or material wealth. A legacy is about planting seeds in a garden you never get to see. I want my children to learn the importance of *get-to-it-of-ness* by thinking of a problem, formulating a plan and putting things into action. Slow motion is better than no motion and better than getting stuck in mental traffic.

I no longer want to be the girl who is afraid to speak up. I want to be the one who speaks with authority, compassion and wisdom. Like those of you who are reading this book, I want everything that I deserve and more. Consequently, I am willing to take the risk to speak. The reward of the risk is simply being too honest and to set an example for those who are watching and listening who have not yet been activated to act.

I know it sounds crazy. For this reason, writing a book about talking is an opportunity to empower others and to pour life into those who may think that their voices do not matter. It's one of the most fundamental things that we do every day in order to live. The quality of our talk will determine the quality of our life. When we decree and declare positive results over our lives, we speak life into our situation. I wanted to examine what it meant to decree and declare.

According to *Dictionary.com*, the definition of decree includes "a formal and authoritative order, especially having the force of law, a judicial decision or order." Oxford dictionary definition includes, "a mandate, proclamation, edict, command, an official order issued by a legal authority". Other definitions include "to state emphatically to show, reveal or manifest and to declare one's position in a controversy." Job 22:28 states, "Thou shalt also decree a thing and it shall be established unto thee: and the light shall shine upon thy ways." Many of us have probably seen these definitions before. We have read them often, but do we truly understand the power of what this word means?

Just as the dictionary provides us with guidance, so do our religious texts. Specifically, Proverbs 18:21 further reminds us that the tongue has the power of life and death. Just as God spoke everything into existence, we as His children have powerful weapons in our words. We can declare blessings or success upon our lives and others. We can cancel out doubt, stress and anxiety in our prayers. Decrees cause the truths of the heavenly realm to manifest into the physical realm. We decree healing when we are sick. We decree provision and abundance when we are lacking. We decree peace when there is turmoil. But it is important to SPEAK! If we do not speak for ourselves then we become vulnerable to others speaking for us and creating our narratives.

To understand this, let's look at the definition of decree. It is "a statement of truth that carries the authority of a court order." A decree is an official order issued by a legal authority. In a prayer "Thy will be done on earth as it is in heaven". Decrees allow truths from the Word and the heavenly realm to be manifested in our earthly realm. In Hebrew, decree means "to divide, separate and destroy." When we decree for example, we must remember the question: "Whom shall I fear?" Based on Psalm 27, we establish peace while separating from anything purposely against it by the enemy and destroying his plans against us. We have the authority to expect to see our words manifested into our life. When we hear, receive and act we have the power to decree the Word. We must be careful to decree what is just and what is right and not our own desires that lead to unfulfillment. Namaste spoken means peace. World peace begins with inner peace. This is our gift to the world. Namaste.

Understanding that we have the power to speak life or death into our own lives and the lives of others, we must think about what is getting in the way. Why don't we have peace? We are not only stewards of our own lives, but we are called to serve as a support for others. I believe this feeling of uneasiness when we are uncomfortable signals or guides us to explore our own thoughts, beliefs and perspectives. We have a unique opportunity to alter the trajectory of our success simply by what we say and the actions that those words manifest. We are accountable for each other by first knowing what it is that we need for ourselves.

If we look at the world around us—current and historical events—there are a few topics that can help to better illuminate this concept. Poverty, specifically, from a financial perspective is one way to explain a current situation or mindset. However, my personal experience and hardest challenge has not centered on poor finances but upon poor perspective. Poverty of mindset has led me to take the comfortable route and not to think outside of the box.

Let me explain further. For many of us, an impoverished mindset is where we believe the worst and take in all the negative talk others have spoken into our lives. Unlike negative self-talk that we can control, we can't control the words or deeds of others. What we can control is how we respond. Thus, the problem of not speaking up is that others start to feel like they can treat you however they want based on what they think is best for you. You may think they are taking your power, but in reality, you are giving it to them because you are not speaking directly. When you start asserting yourself and speaking up, there will be a shift from a poverty to a prosperity mindset.

How to Find Your Voice

I will discuss this in greater detail in another chapter, but for now, I want to share how I find and maintain my voice. Every night, I pray for a discerning spirit. I pray for wisdom and discernment. For context, let's look at Solomon in the Bible. Solomon was a leader who had to make decisions that impacted families and generations to follow. Wisdom is only effective when it is put into action.

A Sunday school lesson from the first book of Kings, Chapter 3 tells the story of Solomon who was a wise king who had to make a decision about maternity. Two women were disputing who was the real mother of a baby. The story shares that both women living in the same house had babies at the same time. One baby died in their sleep. When one mother woke up, she noticed that her baby was dead and unrecognizable. She believed the babies were switched in the middle of the night. When they went to King Solomon, he asked for a sword and gave the order to "Cut the living child in two and give half to one and half to the other," The woman whose son was alive was filled with compassion; she said to the king to give the baby to the other woman and not to kill him. The other woman said, "neither one of us shall have him, cut him in two." King Solomon gave the baby to the one who asked him to stop. The power of life was birthed through having a conversation. King

Solomon's settlement of this dispute brought justice through his discerning heart.

Solomon is a great example of how the tongue and the words we speak carry power and like any power, we must be careful and intentional in how and when we use it. I want everything that God has in store for me, and today I choose me. I am disabling my mute button, and I want to give you the tools I have used in order to make an impact through my use of words. The audacity to speak is simply giving yourself permission to be yourself. Every day of our lives we have to make decisions. Two choices are to either live our best life or to compromise our values. Taking a risk to benefit yourself is sometimes viewed as selfish, but it can be necessary. But what happens if you constantly compromise yourself into situations or arrangements that do not benefit you? You become stressed, weighed down and depressed. Our purpose in life is to thrive and to live life in abundance. Holding yourself hostage because you feel paralyzed to use the power of your voice will keep you in an unproductive space that may feel like a prison.

The opposite of being imprisoned is having audacity. Audacity is defined as a willingness to take bold risks—bold risks with the outcome of peace. Peace of mind and spirit comes when you know that you have done your very best. Booker T. Washington shared that "Excellence is to do a common thing in an uncommon way." In other words, I challenge you to be bold, be risky, be you!

In order to shift your mindset to be bold, first you have to learn to be confident. Having confidence is supported by simply monitoring your own self talk and protecting yourself from the negativity around you. Once you have the ability to be bold, now it's time to speak up.

Communication with our words is one of our most strategic gifts. Talking and listening to children does lots of important things. It improves your bond with others and encourages them to listen to you. It helps them to form relationships and to build self-esteem. Talking has at least two points. First, it conveys messages. Second, it conveys one's willingness to utter and listen to messages. For the latter purpose, small talk is important. But it all begins with how you talk to yourself. This is called self-talk.

There is a simple, yet powerful children's story that illuminates what self-talk is and what it can do. In *The Little Engine That Could*, a simple phrase stating "I think I can. I think I can" was the catalyst for his success. In the tale, a long train needs to be pulled over a very high mountain after its engine breaks down. Larger engines are asked to pull the train; for various reasons, they all refuse. The request is sent to a small engine that agrees to try. The engine knows its limitations, but it engages in self-talk that does not focus on limitations, but possibilities. As a result, it succeeds in pulling the train over the mountain while repeating the motto: "I think I can."

Four simple words propelled the little train into the realm of mighty legends. Sure, you have probably heard this story hundreds of times before, but have you ever paused to really think about its lesson? The story of the little engine has been told and retold many times. The underlying theme is the same.

A stranded train is unable to find an engine willing to take it over difficult terrain to its destination. Only the little blue engine is willing to try and, while repeating the mantra "I think I can. I think I can," he overcomes a seemingly impossible task.

We all can learn from this classic tale, no matter how old we are or what positions we hold in life. As it neared the top of the grade, which had so discouraged the larger engines, it went more slowly. However, regardless of the circumstances, the little blue engine still kept saying, "I—think—I—can, I—think—I—can." It reached the top by drawing on bravery and then went on down the grade, congratulating itself by saying, "I thought I could, I thought I could."

We can learn from countless stories of our childhood that taking risks that support your values and self-worth always ends with positive outcomes. Therefore, audacity is then defined as being bold and confident. Ask yourself when was the last time you made a bold choice or move? How did you feel? What was the outcome? How did others treat you after? Take the time to assess how your moves affect your own self-concept and how others treat you in response to your beliefs and behaviors.

Execution and Action

After understanding that the first step is to be bold, it is important to note that you then have to act. Speaking up and communicating your wants and needs is the only way to get your desired results. It is the foundation for having the audacity to speak.

We learn as babies how to communicate with the world. A baby's first classroom is in their mother's womb. The way you were taught to communicate or to be pacified can block your ability to be soothed, fed, or changed. Before using your words, speaking up for yourself was instrumental in your ability to thrive.

When I was a kindergarten teacher, I knew that I would never win my students' trust by forcing them to be quiet because they had a natural desire to talk. Who was I to stop their flow? Understanding their developmental need to express themselves, I read books to them that affirmed their beliefs and thinking. It led to my research while becoming a literacy specialist on how to develop literate conversations in a kindergarten classroom. I knew the power of talking in my room and adding it to every part of instruction.

One of my favorite read aloud books in my kindergarten class was Tomie de Paola's *Mice Squeak, We Speak*. Simplicity is the soul of Shapiro's toddler-friendly poem about the different ways that animals and humans communicate. The animals and their sounds are each depicted in a series of gaily bordered portraits that include just enough detail to suggest each critter's habitat. The students understood that animals talk to each other but sound different from us. They learned about the different sounds that animals make to communicate with each other. I compared that to the terms of human communication I talk about, specifically, what I speak and what I say.

Let me remind everyone who is reading this: beloved, you are loved, and you are special. Every gift and talent bestowed onto you has been ordained and designer made. No one can be you! Only you can unlock the greatness that you are destined to achieve. Humanity and the world as we know it is depending on you to free yourself of the traps that we put ourselves into by being quiet. Having the audacity to speak is about speaking up because *you* matter.

Like the story about the little engine and the animals in *Mice Squeak, We Squeak*, I also fondly remember the movie *The Wizard of Oz* and watching Dorothy's first encounter with the lion on her way to the Emerald City. The Cowardly Lion sang a song about being afraid. He wondered, "If I only had the nerve."

I wonder how many things we limit ourselves to because we don't have the courage or the heart to achieve. Although we are not following a yellow brick road, there is a path or journey that we are all on. All of our needs are met and the recipe for thriving is already inside each of us.

If we position ourselves to see things positively and affirmatively, we understand that the hardest conversations are the ones that never happen. We are so afraid to speak our mind because we fear the risk of the truth. Once you become fearless, life becomes limitless. Everything that we want and desire lies within us. If we do not speak up for ourselves, our perspectives, thoughts, gifts and talents will be lost and never shared. This missing piece of interaction could have an impact on not only our mental and spiritual health but those around us who are dependent on the power of our voice. We are only competing with who we were yesterday. What will you say today?

I won't spend the time wondering where your mute button was enabled. However I will ask you to reflect on who told you that your voice didn't matter and then say to yourself: *My voice needs to be heard.*

Most recently, COVID-19 has given us new ways of interacting with each other. When someone is speaking virtually and we can't hear them, we remind them that they are on mute. The host then makes sure that they are all muted for background noise and the spotlight is put on the one speaking. How many times have you begun something but haven't been able to hear it? How many times have you placed yourself on mute? Remember, relationships matter, and in order to sustain our relationships with others, we must communicate openly and authentically. No one knows how to treat you unless you tell them.

Whether we are in the midst of a pandemic or we are back to 'normal,' I believe we enter a lot of relationships with a representative and not our true selves because we haven't taken the time to assess what we really need and want for ourselves. Assuming that others will be able to fill those spaces of uncertainty, low self-esteem or value will always restrain a feeling of hopelessness or create an empty feeling. We look to others and things to give us the desired feelings that we need to learn to provide for ourselves. We can't pour into others' lives from an empty place.

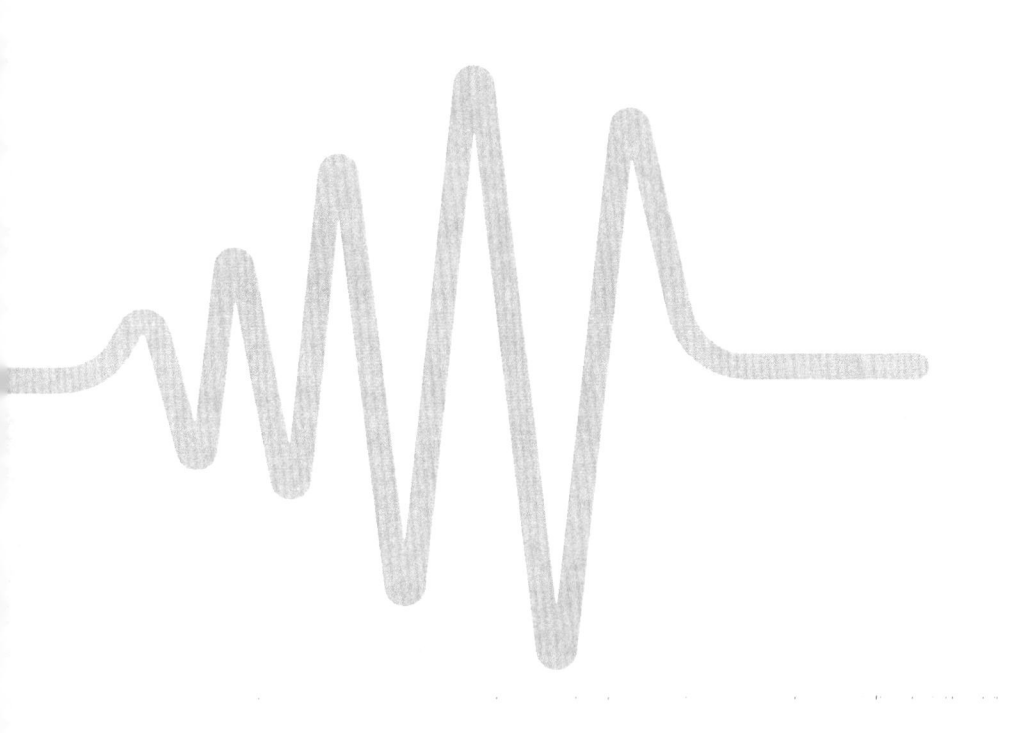

—CHAPTER 2—

Transactional or Transformational

The other day, I ran some errands. As I passed my money to the cashier, I noticed that our exchange was quick and uneventful. I did not catch the name of the cashier, nor did he ask for mine. Although the exchange was pleasant and simple, on a granular level, there was no need to be in a relationship with the cashier.

This exchange is illustrative of a transactional relationship. They rely on a give and take structure. Systems are set so that they give us a sense of reciprocity. However, the trouble is that there has to be a sense of trust established. We are left with always wondering if others are willing to put in the same effort. Often relationships dissolve when one person in a relationship feels that they are constantly outputting energy, time, money, or content without having anything to show in return. Transactional relationships can be what is needed as long as the purpose has been explicitly clear. I wonder how many times we enter into transactional relationships because we are afraid to be vulnerable. When we are vulnerable, we are able to require quality and to tell a story without a feeling of any humanistic touch. Transactional relationships value rules, productivity and organization. The trouble with just having transactional relationships is that they feel like an exchange, which is similar to conducting business. A transactional relationship is when couples treat marriage as a business deal. However again, if this is your style, it is important to understand if the boundaries have been made clear so that no one person is left feeling unheard or unseen.

Myles Munroe reminds us that "When purpose is not known, abuse is inevitable". Relationships that we have with others can either be transactional or transformational. Having a clear purpose about our interactions, relationships or agreements are important to establish in order to reduce disappointment and unmet expectations. When we are unclear about the role someone plays in our lives, we set ourselves up to be unkind to ourselves and those who interact. Being our true authentic selves should always be the goal. When we make this the goal, we can pivot to transformational relationships.

Transformational relationships lead us to evaluate our value, beliefs and behavior. Understand that it is good to constantly evaluate situations based on our real time needs and wants. It takes courage to live in our truth to always be ourselves and not our "representative". Our goal should always be to continue to evolve into a better self. Transformational relationships set a tone for valuing one's beliefs and scaffold opportunities for growth. Communication is key once you have set expectations and collaborative outcomes.

Some relationships that we enter can either grow us or "glow" us. Meaning some people who come into our lives will help us learn something about ourselves and bring out the best. For example, watching my sons train for soccer weekly, I am amazed to see how practice is more important than the game. Each time they are learning a new skill and anticipating possible plays. I know the development of the skill and footwork will always lead to a successful experience on game day. However, it's key to have the right team. No matter how good we practice alone, we still need a team. My hope in beginning any conversation is that we take responsibility and reflect our thoughts of ourselves onto other people. This displacement of energy can lead to positive or negative consequences. The goal is understanding yourself and taking accountability for your shortcomings and facing your fears.

In the report, *Are They Really Ready to Work?* Employers note that although oral and written communication are among the top four skills they seek in new hires, all graduates are lacking in these areas. High school graduates fare the worst with 72 percent of employers citing this group's deficiency in the category "Writing in English," and 81 percent citing their deficiency in the category "Written Communications." Almost half of employers said employees with two-year degrees were still lacking skills in these two areas, while over a quarter of employers felt four-year graduates continued to lack these skills.

I always think about windows, doors and mirrors when interacting with others. A window gives us an opportunity to see beyond ourselves to see what is possible. A door provides opportunities to go outside our comfort zone and to be in spaces that grow us. Mirrors are opportunities that give us space to see ourselves authentically. How are you showing up and questioning what you see? Each of these metaphors help us to be mindful of how our words and actions impact other people. Some people we meet help us to see ourselves differently like a mirror, see other perspectives similar to looking out of a window, or take us to new places out of our comfort zone like walking through a door. Either way we examine our relationships, it is important to learn how to make the initial connections, especially if we desire to have a long lasting, substantive relationship personally or professionally with others.

Before we can even explore being bold enough to speak, it is important to believe that we have the authority to speak life over ourselves. Being muted, or unable to speak is a concern for three reasons. First, when you don't share your thoughts or feelings, you can't be heard. Secondly, no one will know how to interact or to add value to our lives or situation. Also, our gifts and talents cannot be cultivated. Lastly, we are not given space to make meaningful connections with others and to truly be in community with others. That is truly the only way to get what you need. There is power when we give ourselves authentically.

Whether literally or figuratively, being on mute inhibits your ability to share your feelings, concern, or opinion. Communication is the single most important thing that we can use in articulating our thoughts and emotions. How we say it and how we prepare it both impact the trajectory of our life and impact the legacy we leave for generations to come.

When you lack the audacity to speak, you are communicating to others that you don't value yourself enough to be heard. People respond to you the way that you show them how to handle you. Having the audacity to speak also gives life to the talents and gifts that are inside of you. Your ordained gifts to the world have to be unearthed in order to birth the greatness and imagination of the situation for someone else. There is someone whose life can be saved by the power of your words.

Choosing how you show up in a relationship depends on you fully knowing what the desired outcome is that you want. Often you can feel not valued in a transactional relationship because someone is trying to get something out of you. But if you are not clear about your why, you can be left hurt, confused and unheard. Cultivating transformational relationships benefits us all to live an elevated experience of growth and maturity.

Think about your dreams, your interests, and be curious. In fact, think about a specific dream that you've recently had. When we take that stance, we understand that everyone around us has the capacity to help us to get to where we need to be. If we are attentive and authentic, we can sustain a conversation long enough to extract what is necessary in order to move forward. I believe difficult conversations arise when we stay stuck in a place of not expecting the unexpected.

CHAPTER 3

~

Conversational Intelligence

Communication is simply the science of connecting. I believe that every conversation counts because it gets us closer to connecting with others to heal, inform or encourage. We all have a desire to be heard, then have our views shared and accepted. The problem we face often is that we do not know how to overcome roadblocks in communication because we lack confidence, skills or experience. Understanding the science behind a conversation is the fundamental key to unlocking the code of connection. A conversation can be defined as a talk, especially an informal one, between two or more people in which news and ideas are exchanged. In this exchange, there is a desire to be seen and heard. But what happens when we get stuck, or we feel paralyzed when something feels off? It's time to explore and transform the way we think about the interactions that happen with others.

One of my favorite books to read about this topic is *Conversational Intelligence* by Judith Glaser. Glaser's text explores how great leaders build trust and get extraordinary results. She contends that our instinctual need to protect ourselves keeps us from showing up authentically. However, the same signal in our brain that experiences fear and anxiety is also similar to excitement. Glaser learned a powerful, yet, familiar phrase: "Expected the Unexpected" (184). This phrase taught her to reframe fear into curiosity. Anytime we choose to speak to others, it's an opportunity to shift our current situation. Sometimes change is necessary, and the only way to move into a new realm of understanding is to believe that "change can be a door to a new future or can anchor us to the past."

Glaser states that "to get to the next level of greatness depends on the quality of the culture, which depends on the quality of relationships, which depends on the quality of conversations. Everything happens through conversation." (61) She helped me to understand that without conversations our ability to evolve, develop, and innovate drastically diminishes. Once we master the science of a conversation, uncover patterns, remain in the moment, we can then engage in sustainable relationships that build capacity for growth, healing, and acceptance.

The ability to connect, navigate and grow with others is not always an easy one—there is no handbook. Talk is a part of our brain and expands parts of our brain to know what is happening around us. Research conversation forms new DNA that supports to elevate our brains to another part of our being. Language triggers our brain to activate; it can shut down, it can cause introspection to connect, or it can trigger chemistry which brings forth trust. When that happens, we grow our intelligence. The ability to share language that can empower others is the legacy that we leave with others. Over time, when we all are deliberately engaged in these types of conversations, we leave a lasting impact on communities.

One single conversation can trigger an idea that can change a person's life forever. Glaser, over the life of her career, tracked conversations and noticed lives that were changed. "As each person became transparent about their aspirations and intentions to co- create and also what was threatening them, their fears and 'stories' about what was going on, they 'felt a release inside.'" (188) There are billions of neurons waiting to connect to learn new things. Habit patterns limit what we do, so we don't take risks.

This brings me back to the Munroe quote near the beginning of this chapter. Sometimes when the purpose of a thing is not communicated, abuse is inevitable. We have something to learn every day. Every day is an opportunity to add to our tool kit of communication skills. Whether you serve in law, education, health or any other profession that requires you to communicate, it's important to understand that we need each other, and when we are attuned to each other we can set norms and calibrate.

The key to understanding the science of a conversation is to be vulnerable and open to the possibility that we might discover ideas that we never thought of before or confirm a question or feeling that someone might have been pondering. These instances or shifts in interactions create new pathways of growth and great anticipation for the next interaction.

When we create space for others, we give life to parts of ourselves that can be discovered. I believe the success of the Clubhouse app is a great example of how one simple topic and connection can leave others wanting to be in a good space for hours. All it takes is one brave soul to post a topic and to give others the platform to be recognized and to unmute. Glaser shares that co-creating provides "inner spaces" (pg. 185) where our minds need to be free to connect with others in new ways. Through her work as a coach and researcher, there is an understanding that conversations can transform who we are, our relationships, our work environments, and our ability to succeed.

In Glaser's, *Conversational Intelligence*, she states that when "we feel trust, we really open a door that leads to an exchange of thoughts, feelings and dreams with someone else." (12) The opposite is when we feel like someone is a threat, we block anything new into our life increasing anxiety, stress and isolation.

Overall the ability to connect with others helps to navigate and grow with others. Activating the part of your brain to discover and to expand to hold more complex ideas and thoughts helps these frameworks and connections grow over time. Conversations help to impact our ability to shift our brain to a higher language and frequency when we trigger each other to ease fear and to truly thrive. Connecting, being transparent with others uninhibited helps us to build a chemistry to trigger trust. The head and the heart help us to grow our intelligence. Understanding this work helps us to learn, grow and navigate through interactions.

Having the audacity to speak, enables us to have meaningful connections with others. These connections help us to stay curious and compassionate. Things that we say can create physical, emotional reactions in others. Having that understanding, it is important to have an awareness around the things that we say. Physical and chemical reactions are triggered by our words. Understanding the statement that words can hurt or heal is so true. Conversational Intelligence honors what happens inside of us that tries to figure out interactions with others. Success comes from having an awareness of how we relate with each other.

Glaser's study of words revealed that there are some keys that have a feeling of love and connection in the limbic brain in less than .07 seconds. Our brains mark and anticipate the environment that you are in and how the physical environment relates. Often people feel excluded in the immersion process which teaches how to decipher how leaders need to be prepared for contrast change. Making the invisible visible to be our best selves. Part of the job of a leader is to be conscious of how we are showing up and to be accountable for our feelings. Once a leader acknowledges and adds value and touches other's hearts, they will connect love with others. Showing appreciation is key when leading others in any capacity. This leads to a great motivation of others and an example of what can be possible.

Every interaction with others should go through an audit process inquiring whether your conversation would help to build trust or delude trust. Many therapists and coaches believe that trust is the foundation for every connection. Distrust causes us to emotionally go into fight or flight mode creating messages that can be unclear. Conversational Intelligence helps to bring others into trust. Integrity, empathy, wisdom, strategy insight and foresight are the residue of defining trust. Positional power comes from roles not being clear and others not feeling appreciated. The same way we build trust with others is the same for ourselves. Assessing your own self talk is important to establish ways to connect. I will continue to explore how to build trust and enable them to be their best selves. The author, Judith Glaser, argues that humans are wired to be profoundly impacted.

—CHAPTER 4—

Examining Talk and Trust

Whether it's talking to yourself, spouse, partner, another adult, or God, there are key things to keep in mind that will allow you the opportunity to get what you want. What we think is one thing, but what we do and how we act next is the only thing that counts. Proverbs 14:23 reads "All hard work brings a profit, but mere talk leads only to poverty." The goal of every interaction is to advance. However, it can be difficult to connect with others when your past traumas get in the way. So many of us stay on mute for fear of rejection, lack of confidence or simply not knowing how to even begin. The key in any industry or relationship is to create a space for others to feel seen and heard. It is that simple.

Think to yourself for a moment and reflect on what is the hardest thing for you to say: I apologize, I need help, I love you, I am sorry, Thank you, Yes or No? Your answer to this question might reveal the first key that is needed to unlock your unlimited possibilities of being your true authentic self. Your past is just that—behind you! It's time to forgive your past and to live in the present so that your future will reap the opportunities of all that you will sow now. Having the audacity to speak will benefit you now and later. Your life not only depends on it, but your legacy requires for you to walk in your own truth. Today, I made the choice to be bold and to speak up. You can do the same because you matter!

Whether you're an artist, student, teacher, minister, transit worker, entrepreneur, or politician, you have to use your words. Our position or status in life does not determine our power. Our words determine our lives. In short, if you have life in your body, embracing the audacity to speak is specifically for you. It provides a key to understand that every interaction is an opportunity to get closer to your dreams and goals.

By now, you may feel some trepidation, especially if you are shy or introverted. Don't worry if you are thinking that this may be difficult for you. Over time, the way you speak to yourself will improve. Your relationships with others will be intentional. In turn, the way others treat you will be rewarding. If the world learned to speak to each other our lives would improve, communities would flourish, and our world would be a kinder place.

Everyone knows that first impressions are important, but you would be surprised about how long it takes to make a first impression. Within the first seven seconds of meeting, people will have a solid impression of who you are, and some research suggests a tenth of a second is all it takes to start determining traits like competence and trustworthiness. If during the first seven seconds you already make a decision, trust happens; then it is crucial to decide what you will do with the opportunity once you land a chance to develop a relationship.

I once watched a video of Joyce Meyers where she stated, "We can improve our relationships with others by leaps and bounds if we become encouragers instead of critics." This quote is a powerful one that reminds us that our relationships can either be a launching pad or an impenetrable boulder when it comes to our audacity to speak.

There is one definite fact about life, we will at some point have an interaction with someone. This interaction will either meet our expectations or disappoint. I am a firm believer that I want to leave people feeling better about life after being around me.

The purpose of Audacity to Speak is to equip you with the tools needed to have a conversation that will lead to better relationships and outcomes aligned with your personal or professional values and desired life goals. Every relationship is reciprocal and having the ability to organize your thoughts, beliefs, and desires helps to achieve higher predictive and life fulfillment. It all begins with pushing past your fears and having the confidence to trust yourself. Knowing what you want is inherent. Knowing how to speak up is a skill that I will address later in the book.

Communicating clearly is one of the key standards for all of us, not just students. Having the ability to articulate thoughts and ideas effectively using oral communication skills in a variety of forms and contexts shapes one's ability to inform, instruct, promote values, examine attitudes and intentions while motivating and the ability to persuade.

I often wonder about what holds me back from speaking or sharing what is on my mind. As I shared in chapter one, I can vividly remember Ms. Tillman reprimanding me in first grade telling me to be quiet and that I talked too much. We also know that children were taught to speak when spoken to or to be seen and not heard, but how does that work as adults now? As a child I wasn't taught that my voice mattered and that I was worthy of being included. The environments that we curate for others should always include everyone. That is true inclusivity.

In business, unions that fight for the collective bargaining rights of its members are given a platform and told that their voice matters. In 2020, the pharmaceutical and healthcare industry in the United States spent the most on lobbying efforts, totaling to about 306.23 million U.S. dollars. That is a lot of time, effort and money spent on persuading someone to do something. When I had the opportunity to lobby in New York State, I had to come prepared with a list of questions that I wanted answered along with some clear next steps that I would want to implement. Had I not been prepared, it would have been a missed opportunity to use my voice to advocate for something I believed in.

Much like the attention that we pay to our professional and personal lives we must also think about how our words feed our spirit. Spiritual audacity reveals itself when we reflect on how God communicates with us. Depending on your faith, it is a form of spiritual audacity; it empowers us to have the confidence to speak when we are unable to do so on our own. While faith seeks understanding, it does not always help us to understand the providential ways of God. The confidence of the believer is born of the conviction that God is utterly trustworthy in character and promise, and this generates deep humility.

Our relationship with providence becomes clearer when we consider prayer which requires us to articulate our desires. When we pray, we ask for forgiveness, we extend our gratitude, we petition for others, we ask for ourselves and we close in reverence of him. God knows what we need before we ask him. Having faith doesn't eliminate problems and tragedies from our life. It means that providence ultimately finds its appropriate response in praise. Yet if we don't have the courage to seek, we will not find it. Simple, have the audacity to speak even to God.

Understanding the purpose of what you need, and your goals is the centerpiece for any interaction. The desires of your heart can only be granted if you share authentically with others and make things clear. Everything is right about showing up as your true authentic self. Living life in community with each other is the key to our success.

The foundation of all relationships is trust. Trust fuels the momentum of a conversation to be productive or to fail. I believe the three areas that we have to examine are our concept of ourselves, what motivates us and the impact of traumatic experiences. Understanding how you are responsible for how you show up is significant in being able to grow. If you are unclear about your own self-motivation and trauma, you can spiral into a place of depression, feeling lost or not included. This may result in severing healthy relationships or pushing away people who genuinely love and care about you.

I have studied over the course of academic studies in college the impact of childhood when examining trust and being vulnerable. Examining the psychology of communication is vital in having the audacity to speak.

I have been intrigued by psychology which provided an understanding around behavior. I believe it is important to examine psychology theorists when examining trust. Without trust, connections to others can be difficult and relationships will not last. Specifically, understanding the impact of trust over a lifespan, the value of self would be held in high esteem along with accepting others.

The Ego and Child Development

Sigmund Freud was a human psychologist specializing in personality theory, and in 1923 he saw Id, the ego and the superego all developing at different ages of our lives. These systems in our mind serve as a focus of behavior. According to his psychosocial belief, the ego is the realistic part that works between our primitive mind and fantasy. Our personality develops over time but begins early. How we communicate to urges and needs is established early as a baby. It's the unconscious pleasure principle; impulses should be satisfied and get satisfied. The ego is the part that has been influenced by the external world; it mediates and is the decision making by reason. The ego is the reality principle and protects to avoid negative consequences. Rules and consequences are in constant decision making. Self-control comes from our development of our ego.

As it relates to this, trust is developed over time as a child interacts with their environment. This is why I believe bonding with your baby and potty training is crucial to the overall adjustment of children. They grow to have trusting relationships and can let things go. Teaching new moms how to communicate early with their baby is one of the most important features of raising a little one.

The importance of ego in childhood helps to establish secure relationships and to develop a positive sense of self. I believe that Freud would agree that our first attachments and environmental circumstances impact trust. Trust then serves as a learned behavior from your relationships and environment.

Maslow and Motivation

Maslow was another leading thought expert who wanted to focus on human development. His hierarchy of needs theory is my point of reference when interacting with anyone at any age. Utilizing the pyramid as shown, helps you to navigate any situation to help others to achieve self- actualization. Achieving that is critical to feel the need to belong, feel safe, feel a sense of love and esteem all to achieve self- actualization. Our motivation then increases as needs are met. Our habits of mind supported by our environment helps us to mature and grow over time. Maslow's focus was on human potential and how we can be our best.

As I share with educators and families alike, before anyone can tap into the gifts of others or simply connect, you must understand how basic needs must be met first. Pedro Negra states in his writing that you cannot teach a hungry child. This means that if the basic needs of food, shelter and safety are not met, nothing else can begin that will be productive.

In alignment to the bottom half of the pyramid, Maslow also states that love and belonging are a need. Maslow, a humanistic psychologist, believed that we all need to feel loved, to belong to something meaningful, to have purpose and to be happy. Therefore, trust comes from acknowledging the needs of others and creating spaces that help others to thrive. Moving towards the peak reveals self-actualization which is our constant motivation to our human potential. I believe knowing that we all strive towards an intrinsic goal reveals the need for development and support over time. Meaningful connections come from our awareness of our courage and vulnerability. Needs lower down in the hierarchy must be satisfied before individuals can attend to needs higher up. Questions to ask may include: Am I safe? Do I have what I need for food, clothing and/or shelter? Can I earn what I need to live to survive? Do I feel loved by family or friends? Do I feel worthy?

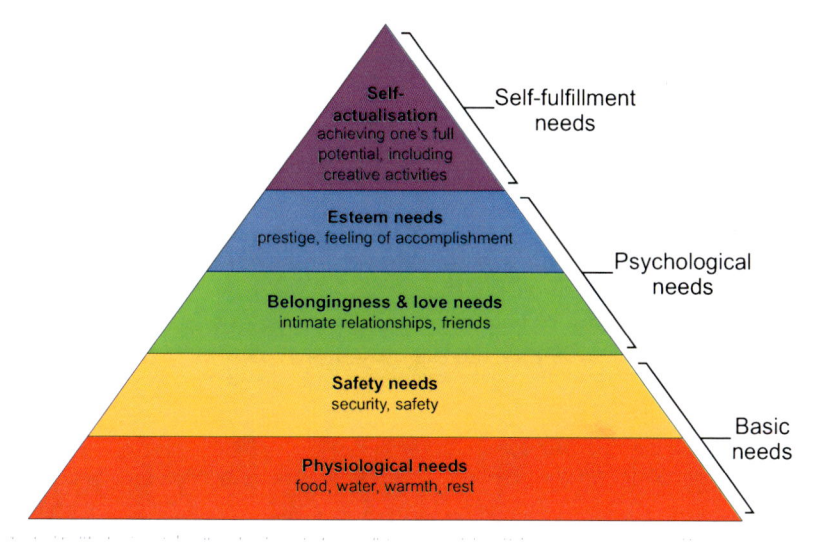

Source: https://commons.wikimedia.org/wiki/File:Maslow%27s_Hierarchy_of_Needs2.svg

Developmental Lifespan Stages and Affirmations

In every stage of our life, we are inherently figuring things out. While we figure things out, our decisions are made based on our current understanding of our projected needs and desires that will impact our future. Psychologist Erik Erikson created a lifespan theory of significant moments at each stage of our lives. Unlike other theorists who focus on child development, Erikson described identity as something that shifts and changes throughout a lifespan and that our self-image is created by experiences, relationships, beliefs and values. I believe it is important to know your age and your stage. Each level has a self-talk affirmation that would be helpful in order to thrive. When preparing to speak to others I believe we should approach others with a sense of curiosity. Adding value to others has to begin with an acknowledgement where others are emotionally, spiritually or mentally. Exploring these areas helps to understand your current psychological development. It is human to question your sense of self or place in the world, it is compassionate to understand that life is a process and we as a community stand in service to each other's development.

Stages and Affirmations:

1-18 months The caregiver is the centerpiece of a child developing trust. Voice is critical to establishing connections with a little one. Singing to your child and bonding leads to a happy baby. Establishing routine is another important feature in developing trust. This trusting bond will last a lifetime and will be the foundation for every relationship that will follow. Anxiety and stress come when children do not feel safe in their environment, and they don't trust that the outcome will be soothing. It is critical to communicate and to speak to build a trusting and connected relationship. Hope comes from an expectation that a desired action will follow. The caregiver has a responsibility to be seen, heard and felt.

Affirmations to Say/ Sing: Say the baby's name over and over again with a song. Say I love you! Singing nonsense words and rhymes are fun and enjoyable to have the little one to show emotions and to laugh! Joy is the goal!

18 months- 3years: This stage is always connected to the terrible twos and threes, and I would say this is the best time to build resilience and grit out of children. The will to do something is nurtured at this age and stage. I love when children are able to learn to command and to use their voice. I often celebrate hearing the word NO! Often yes, children learn to communicate through their somewhat aggressive behaviors, but having the ability to communicate and to use their voice becomes a game changer. Children learn to succeed through having their needs met while learning self-control and to condition when things are allowed through a supportive environment. Learning to use the bathroom independently is a critical piece to learning to let things go. There is a sense of accomplishment and dignity that is attached to using the bathroom independently. Children begin to learn control over their bodies, which is important when interacting with other children. The environment plays

an integral part of this stage. The environment should be set to allow children to explore and to try things without risk of failure in order to build the stamina to try again independently and with guidance.

Affirmations to be said: I love you. I see you. I hear you. You are safe. I am here. Try this! Use your words! You Did IT! Everything is Right About You!

Age 4: This stage is a critical time in a child's life where they learn the power of discovery. The BEST way to discover is to play. Play is a human right that has to be included everywhere. Whether imaginative, or having concrete items, giving children the opportunity to remain curious is so important. This stage is all about students having the ability to question and to assert themselves to try new things. Providing an environment where students choose is key. Social interactions are critical in supporting the ability to express needs and desires. Setting a purpose for the day should be fun and enjoyable.

Affirmations to say and to practice: Tell Me More, What would you like to today? Where would you like to go? I set intentions for my day through talking and playing. I can learn new things every day! I make decisions every day. Everything is Right About Me!

5-12: Teachers play an important role in a child's life in order to teach skills that will be fostered for independence. The key is autonomy. Self-esteem comes from peer groups. Children benefit from learning specific skills to feel accomplished. This will build confidence in order to continue to have the desire to achieve goals that they feel helps to be valued.

Affirmation to say and to practice: I learn as much as I can to be the best that I can! I believe in my potential, not my past! I can do hard things! I stay curious. Everything is Right about Me!

12-18: This stage adolescents are searching to define self and personal identity. The guiding questions are Who am I and Why am I here? How do I or will I fit into society? What do I believe is right and wrong? Morality of a child and the ethics of an adult. I know my place as I continue to evolve.

Affirmations to say: I choose to be the best that I can be to contribute to the life that I dream about because I am exactly where I am supposed to be! I accept myself unconditionally. I am proud of who I am becoming. Everything is Right About Me!

18- 40: This stage can bring the introduction of loving and intimate relationships with others. This is the time to explore long term commitments that are caring and that bring joy. Be curious and compassionate about lessons learned and the impact on your ability to trust. Seeking a coach or therapist would be helpful to have someone to talk things out with about expectations.

Affirmations to say: I am worthy of love. Practice makes permanent! I deserve love. I am open to receiving love. I attract the abundance of love inside of me! Everything is Right About Me!

40 -65: This stage is often considered midlife, questions surface around standing in life. Questions similar to what footprints will be left behind for others to follow or how have I contributed? Being a part of something that has the potential to make a meaningful impact is often the desired feeling. Care is a theme around taking care of others or questioning who will take care of them. This is a good time to join an organization or to start a movement. Think about creating something new!

Affirmation: I believe in my potential, not my past! I let go of my past beliefs that no longer serve me. I make choices that are aligned to my values. Every day I contribute value and meaning. Everything is Right About Me!

65 and up: This stage often can bring sorrow to some and joy for others. This is the time some reflect on life. I believe offering compassion is crucial. There might be some past hurt or guilt. Remind yourself or someone else of the wisdom that you/ they have to offer.

Affirmation: I am wise beyond measure. I contribute in my own special way. I am living the best years of my life. Everything is Right About ME!

CHAPTER 5

Take The Day On

When thinking about how to develop a problem of practice, I wanted to frame my thoughts around an understanding of psychology that I learned in college. My studies at Hampton University as a psychology major afforded me the opportunity to study many different theorists. One that comes to mind was one that serves a practical application to life, Erik Erikson. He believed that at every stage of life we go through a crisis that shapes us where we either get through our situations or stay stuck and left unresolved. Audacity to speak is the understanding that we all have times where we develop and go through challenges in our lives. Developing trust of knowing that everything happens the way it's supposed to then ushers in a renewed sense of "I think I can."

Applying this understanding is important when we step out to speak up. It's important to be mindful of the age and stage of others. Considering where people are emotionally is key in establishing a meaningful connection.

In my recent completion of Leadership with Momentum Education my contract was to be an authentic bold and compassionate leader. The joke was it was really a reminder to myself how I wanted to show up but not necessarily how I truly felt. My age and stage according to Erik Erikson would suggest that I am at the stage of middle adulthood. Each adult must find some way to satisfy and support the next generation. Which totally makes sense that now as a leader mom and wife I have realized that living out my selfish dreams helps to birth the dreams of others around me. The unfortunate part of this is that as Dame would say…. I often stall and don't finish. He shared an example with me in front of my son Sy, sharing as a striker that if he would stall, the opponent would get the ball and score. Taking self-inventory I believe what my coach Fia would say is that comfort and excellence don't go together. So true!

So I found the courage to push and found an incredible executive coach, Dr. Jill, who is now relevant. Learning the Bio Codes has afforded me the opportunity to pace myself to evaluate how I respond and to appreciate the feelings of vulnerability because it's the point of information that provides opportunities to connect.

Depending on whether you are an introvert or extrovert, you have learned unique coping mechanisms to help you to thrive. Personally, I am an introvert with extrovert tendencies. Meaning simply I like being in a group, but I love and feel safer being alone. It hurts when you feel left out. I personally had to deal with moments of feeling that I wasn't included. But then I realized I had to practice confidence and shift the way I saw situations.

Working with Dr. Jill has transformed my life. Having the audacity to speak means that you will be ready to take the day on. The Bio Code system has allowed me to learn practical, actionable, in-the- moment strategies to build your behavioral intelligence with The BioCode System. You will learn how to grow in your environment, in real-life moments, and become stronger than your stress, so life starts to feel easier.

Bio Codes helps me to conquer my comfort zone. When we don't feel empowered to use our voice, we often are left with that uneasy feeling of not being included, seen or heard. When it comes to everyday challenges and challenging people, we are winging it. The missing piece: BioCoding or Behavioral Agility: the ability to consciously choose empowered behaviors regardless of the difficulty of the situation.

What's a Bio Code Moment? How can I catch it? ®

The big idea. I mean the highest-level idea is that every single thing in life is here to help us, not to hurt us. The good, the bad, and the ugly. Everybody wants to live their best life. Everybody wants to be happy, healthy, successful, useful, purposeful. We want to belong to something greater than ourselves. Everybody wants what's good…but then why is the world stressed out?

We're not feeling good about ourselves. We're getting upset, we're getting frustrated in traffic, we're not happy in our jobs. We're unhappy with the states and conditions because there's something missing. What's missing? This…

We were taught what to do when things are going well, but not in the moments when things are not going according to plan. There are not any real-time, real-life strategies in those moments to use stress as an opportunity for us to grow. So the whole premise of The Biocodes System® is to teach an individual how to become behaviorally fit.

In order to do that we have to see where we're not fit, where we can't do this, where we get stressed out, where things trigger us and bother us so that we can learn how to do the work.

An individual learning how to accept one hundred percent responsibility for how they're showing up to meet any challenge, regardless of the situation, regardless of the behaviors of others, frees that individual from being a victim or blaming other people for the situation they're in.

Instead, I see everything as an opportunity to become stronger, to become more behaviorally fit, so that I can show up healthier - with mental clarity, with emotional stability, with kindness and compassion, and create new solutions in a world that's filled with a lot of hard moments.

Most of us have been taught how to overcome challenges in academic and athletic situations, but not human behavior under stress. That's a missing skill set. We learn academic intelligence, but we really don't learn behavioral intelligence. So when stress hits, the common methodology that most people have is to move away from the environment - you meditate, you medicate, you go for a run, you take a nap, take a vacation - you move away from the situation to decompress. All these strategies are great and beautiful for restabilizing away from the moment. However, come Monday morning or that next moment...what you've left behind is waiting for you again.

It becomes a vicious cycle of replenish and deplete, replenish and deplete. The take the day off strategies which we all love and adore are amazing, but The Biocodes System teaches us how to take the day on. Meaning, at 3:54pm when the kid is screaming, the meeting gets canceled, whether I ate organic veggies or not, or meditated...it's probably not going to matter. I'm not going to grab that book off the shelf and say, "wait, this is what's happening to me according to Chapter 5 paragraph 4." Nobody is doing that in moments, real time, real life. So The Biocode System gives you an exercise experience to help you see where life pushes against you, so that you can bring the focus back to yourself, accept full responsibility, see where you are weakening, and use tools to strengthen yourself in real time.

Most people believe that their problem…is the problem. "If I can only get rid of this aspect of my life - if people could only listen to me, if I lost the weight, if I could get the job, if my kids were well behaved - I'll be able to get the things I want; I'll be able to feel good." The belief is that something has to happen, or somebody has to change, or something external to myself has to be fixed before I'll be okay. The Biocode System teaches you that your problems are not the problem. How you're approaching problems is the bigger problem.

Problems are a part of life. They'll always be here. Problems never go away, they just change. If I can reframe the story in my mind, I can say; "My problems are not the biggest problem. The biggest problem is me in it."

Whoa! One hundred percent responsibility. That's a lot! It feels right though. It's something I can work with. Although completely intimidating, in a way, it's a breath of fresh air. I can't control what's happening outside of myself, but I can control myself.

I see now that I never learned how to approach problems from that place of strength and stability - to be able to meet those moments. As I get stronger it gets easier.

You go to the gym and want to get fit, so you have stress - stress all over the place. You pick up a weight that's filled with stress and you don't say "oh, this is stressing me out! I need to put it down so that I can get stronger. I need to get rid of it, let it go, release it so that I can grow." No, you lift it acknowledging that the stronger you get the lighter the weight will feel.

We never learned how to use stress as a strategy for personal growth. This is a bright new way of thinking, and the rest is, "how do I do that?" Without further ado…here's The Biocode System in a nutshell:

Biocode 1 is Self-Empowerment. The concept is to notice a problem, and then bring the focus back to the self. Stabilize before approaching that problem.

I realize now that how I show up to meet the moment is more important than the moment I'm meeting.

I'm an athlete in the gym. I realize now that my tendency was to skip over step 1 and go directly to step 2 - "that's not true, that's not right, that's not what I said." My tendency is to go right into problem solving.

Of course this is totally understandable because we're problem solvers by nature. However, I know now that there's a crucial step to take before problem solving. Bring the focus back to myself. Focus on my own behavior first before I meet that person or that problem.

Biocode 1 is not claiming that problems or stressful things don't exist…it's saying that I have to focus on my behavior so that I can meet the problem, and therefore have more favorable outcomes. The goal is to successfully navigate challenging moments. How do I best do that? Simple. By remembering what I control and focusing on that.

There's a part of me that tends not to want to go inside and recognize the current conditions of my internal world. The part of me that wants to avoid taking one hundred percent responsibility for my feelings, is what holds me back from best navigating challenging moments and having favorable outcomes. Ultimately that part of myself is what's preventing me from living my best life.

Again, the analogy of working out is a good one. The muscle I'm flexing is the neural pathway connection. I look at the stressful situation and decide to bring it back to myself first.

"I'm going to stabilize now. No matter what's happening, I'm consciously deciding how I'm showing up to meet this moment." I'm reprogramming my brain and remembering that it's on me. Every time I do this is the equivalent of lifting a set of weights - making myself stronger so that the stressful situations become lighter.

BioCode 2 focuses on your negative self-talk. It is that story that you have in your head that goes around and around and around. This BioCode teaches you how to stop the unproductive story loops.

Am I in control of my thoughts or are my thoughts in control of me? If your thoughts are in control of you, this is going to change your life forever! BioCode2 stops the negative self-talk, labels the emotion, and then finds the opposite one.

It's amazing to me how quickly this process transforms my emotional state of being. First, I go fishing for weaker thoughts. Once I catch the story, I label it with a one-word emotion to describe how it makes me feel.

Example: I feel frustrated, worried, doubtful.

Step two: adjust. I found the exact opposite word. Pain is my indicator showing me the weak muscle that needs strengthening. Example: frustration\patience, worry\trust, doubt\confidence.

Step three: action. I practiced saying the opposite word at that moment. "I feel frustration, practice patience. I feel worried, practice trust."

It takes repetition and must be done regardless of how you feel or function to get stronger.

What keeps me stuck is dwelling in my weaker emotional words and being judgmental of myself for having negative emotions. What helps is categorizing emotions as negative or positive and then consciously choosing where to focus my attention.

BioCode 3 teaches the timing codes with a focus on regulating emotions. When emotions run high, thoughts and words lie.

When I'm emotional, I may say things I don't really mean. I may do things that I later regret. The only emotional state that I should be in when I'm trying to problem-solve is stable and neutral.

Problems are instruments for personal growth here on this planet, so we want to be very mindful and fact based when we're problem solving. Therefore, we learn how to solve problems in the neutral.

Ever looked at someone who's upset and told them to calm down? Yeah, right! Never in the history of calm down has anybody calmed down. Why? Because there's a time to feel and there's a time to deal. It's never in the same moment.

The third Biocode teaches me when it's the best possible time to solve something. If I'm in an emotional state that's unstable, no good is going to come out of it. Instead of talking about the problem, I'm going to be talking about disappointments and expectations that weren't met.

Biocode 3 is an observational skill where I notice what emotional state myself and others are in. Only by notification can I determine if I should walk, talk, or listen.

I personally have the tendency to engage in dramatic moments even when I'm in an emotionally unstable state. Perhaps the heightened state of conflict serves a desire to feel alive, or simply feels comfortable because of the culture of the household I grew up in. However, I've noticed that it's also caused those who I love to often feel distant from me. That's what I don't want. Although I might engage in disagreement, I never want those I love to feel unloved.

The third biocode teaches me to flex the muscle of patience. It bothers me to ask the question, "is it more important for me to be right, or to have peaceful and kind relationships?"

BioCode 4 focuses on Effortless Communication. One of the biggest problems we have on this planet... is a breakdown of communication – especially when things don't go according to plan. We see it at every level whether in daily routines with our family and coworkers, or in government and international affairs.

How do I behave when I don't see eye to eye - when things don't go according to plan? Biocode 4 teaches me how to see the good intentions behind the dysfunctional words that others might be using. It teaches me to see that it's not meanness, it's weakness.

The truth is that many of us never learned how to appropriately ask for what we want. We never learned how to speak kindly and clearly when stressed. Understanding this on a deep level leads to compassion. Compassion is a total game changer when it comes to communication.

The fourth Biocode teaches me how to translate others' dysfunctional words into functional meaning. What are they trying to say? What are their needs? Only by understanding the answers to these questions will I be able to respond in a way which enhances the connection between us.

The muscle being strengthened is the ability to put messages out better than they came in. I'm learning to speak healthfully – regardless of others' poor communication. I know in my heart that I want, and can, make the right move regardless of how things are said or done.

BioCode 5 is all about self-navigation. How do we navigate the storms of our lives, and go towards and away from things? How can we rebound rapidly and pivot forward?

I'm learning to ask the questions, "how quickly can I leave the past where it belongs…in the past? Can I redirect myself away from things that don't serve me without taking anything personally, or making anyone wrong?"

BioCode 5 teaches me strategies for those moments when things are not going according to plan. How can I deal with the problem, rebound rapidly, and walk out clean to meet the next experience without that whole big mess coming with me?

First, I become aware whenever I feel trapped or stuck... "alright, this doesn't feel so good." Then I ask, "am I really stuck, or do I have the ability to focus forward in a new direction?"

I'm realizing that if I stay flexible and unattached to specific outcomes, that I will move faster and create new possibilities effortlessly. I'm realizing that feeling like I'm the victim and blaming others tends to keep me stuck. I don't want that. I want to feel free. Freedom is my ability to focus forward.

So, there they are... The five codes that make up The BioCode System. Each has a distinct lesson and focus. The first two are only about you, the third one is an observation skill, and the last two are about how we interact in life through communication and self- navigation. All BioCodes are set up the same way. There's a goal and a new perspective. Then there's a three-step process of how to do that exercise: There's a self-awareness step because you can't change what you can't see. There's an adjustment step to apply a new strategy. And, there's an action step to begin practicing the new, more empowered behavior.

To sum it all up, I would say that the Biocodes have helped me most by realizing that when things are not going according to plan, it's an opportunity to grow. I mean it really, really is. The more I've been opening up to this reality, the stronger I find myself getting. I can't tell you how good it feels. I now believe that what my heart wants most is to grow, and that perhaps that's what all of our hearts yearn for progress. As I practice, I'm forming new, stable habits. I'm getting stronger and building a life of health, happiness and inner peace.

Writing this book has been difficult for many reasons but for the sake of time I will narrow it down to three things. First making time to stop to complete. Second, believing that it is possible and lastly not listening to the negative talk of teachers telling me that I wasn't good enough. Once you sum up all of these equal self-doubting parts I realized that it was time to stop relying on others and to push my way into being uncomfortable.

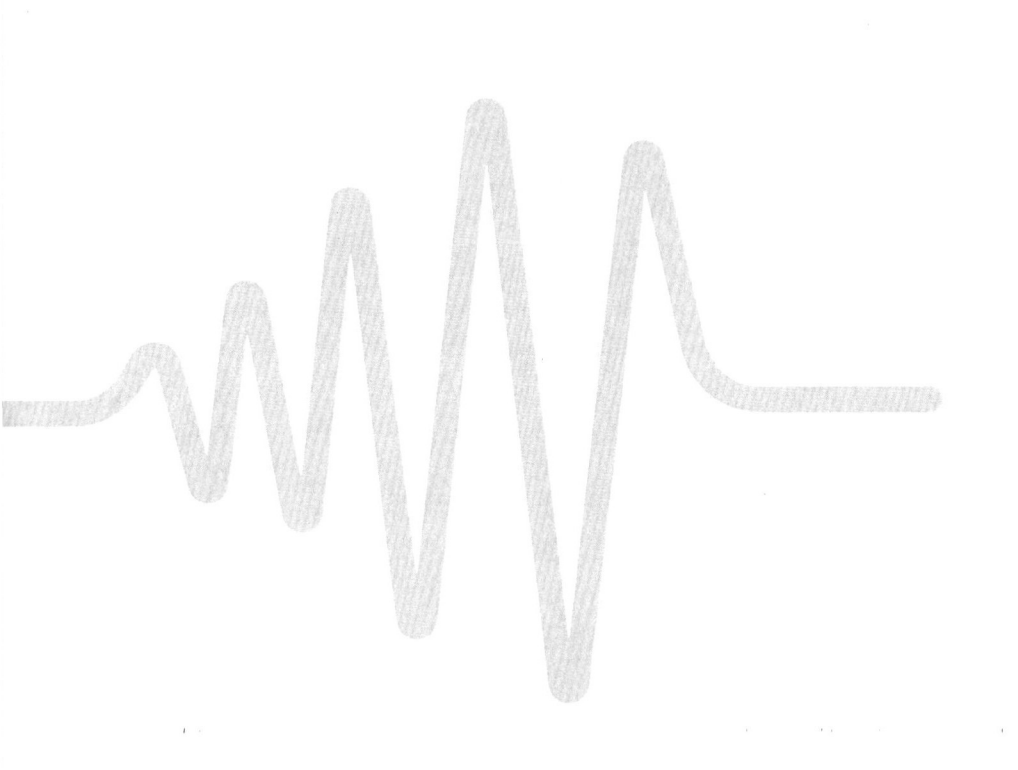

CHAPTER 6

The Results Are In

Sawubona! This Zulu greeting has been one of my favorite phrases. It means "I see you." More than words of politeness, Sawubona carries the importance of recognizing the worth and dignity of each person we see and interact with. All of us matter to God which means we all should matter to each other and that starts with being able to see each other's humanity. Understanding the importance of valuing others supports a genuine and long-lasting connection. This connection supports the ability to show up authentically and to have the audacity to speak.

Showing up for others and holding space to give others a platform creates true authenticity. We have to encourage others to be visible and to show up. I am aware that it is not easy to unmute. However, practice mirrors what is possible. The opportunities that we give ourselves to do hard things helps to build our stamina to overcome anything. We build an internal muscle that helps us to be resilient. Acknowledged deliberate action steps to practice stepping out of our comfort zone bring light to interrupt and disrupt loneliness and to form true connections with others.

Psalm 138:3 states "In the day when I cried out, you answered me, and made me bold with strength in my soul." Speaking even in the Bible, offers clarity around boldly thanking God for the blessings bestowed or for deliverance. Like the psalmist, we must understand that when we are able to speak and to use our voice, we are then able to share our wisdom with others. There is nothing more important than creating a community offering true connections. Specifically, speaking elicits an action that offers an invitation to grow, reveal wisdom or to comfort. If this is true, being bold and speaking up is key to any relationship.

Brené Brown, in her book *Daring Greatly*, shares that "Connection is the energy that is created between people when they feel seen, heard, and valued; when they can give and receive without judgment." When we create vulnerable spaces with grace and compassion, true connections are formed. There is healing in spaces when the environment is set that is judgment free and offers one the opportunity to be themself. Feelings of fear, anxiety and depression begin to appear when we are not given the chance to show up without judgement. Grace does not eliminate consequences. The result of a positive interaction is the possibility of another one.

Every opportunity that I have to interact with someone, I always use it as an opportunity to gain wisdom, connection and to add value. I always take the time to intentionally create opportunities for others to feel seen and heard. I value you because I know how it feels to not be offered an invitation to just be yourself. I have found, for over twenty-five years, that there are three ways to show up authentically. We have the permission to be human. Once we get beyond ourselves, we get to belong to something bigger than ourselves.

Growing up many of us were taught that children were supposed to be seen and not heard. Then we become adults and just like that we have a voice and are asked to speak up. There are years in between the trauma of silencing that occurs when children are not given an opportunity to share how they are feeling or what they are noticing. Adding to the conversation could be around racial battle fatigue that occurs when you are just exhausted from how others treat you based on their own biases. At what point do we have permission to learn how to show up to be ourselves and to offer others the opportunity to add value.

Yes, life is about showing up for yourself and others. Yes, when we show up for ourselves it feels good to be authentic. And yes, it feels good to be in a space where freedom exists. This freedom then opens opportunities to connect with others. When we connect with others and create space for them to be free of any fakeness we then can build on each other's purpose and value that can be rendered. When we listen to connect to others and not reply immediately, others feel safe to share. What we are thinking we will seek out on others. Therefore our interactions with each can trigger exactly what you are looking for to heal, answer a question or to affirm. Your yes by speaking up is attached to a breakthrough in your life or someone else's. Each one of us has the potential to be the catalyst to pull others up and to unlock their potential by just one conversation.

Think about a genuine connection that you have with someone else. How do you feel after you have talked to them? Excited? Motivated? Inspired? I personally feel a true sense of excitement when I can connect with someone in a way that they don't feel pressure to be something that they are not. It feels good to know that when I am around, being yourself is the expectation. If we are truly going to present ourselves in authentic ways, I have found it necessary to always be a light in any situation. The three things that I use as a rubric are ego, humor, and highlight. I have been able to use these three ways of showing up for others to make a meaningful connection. Once a meaningful connection is established, the purpose of your relationship can become clear and open to the endless possibilities.

Unlike what you may have been taught about ego, it is simply taking the time to know a little bit about a person. Their interest, their talent or skill and naming it. I believe making others feel good about themselves is key in any relationship. With the greatness I believe that I have in me, I then honor the greatness in them by saying it. As an example, I would say, I can see that you are exceptional at singing. Tell me more about how you chose this as a career. I would extend the questions depending on the flow of the conversation to elaborate on developing the other's ego.

Acknowledging another's ego brings to light that it's ok for others to honor you and to see you. Often, teaching kindergarten, I learned how important it was to give my five-year-old the opportunity to speak in my class. They had so much to say about themselves and I gave them the floor every time especially when they ended up on a tangent because I knew that their world centered around them. This egocentric undertaking fueled their confidence and helped them to achieve being able to speak up.

Now as a leader, friend, mother, or wife I know I have to value who I come in contact with, and I can do that simply by speaking to their "EGO." If we were to define ego from a psychological perspective, I would describe ego as an internal negotiator finding fair ways of gaining acceptance, power, love, or any other desire without jeopardizing your character and to satisfy both parties.

Every day we make choices that are aligned to our values. Highlighting another's "ideal" self shows that you are a willing participant and are creating a space of vulnerability to show up authentically. Everyone deserves a confidence boost. Life can be hard enough. Showing up and sharing how you appreciate or are interested in something that they are doing is a sure way to begin any relationship. Silencing someone's inner critic and creating a space for them to belong is a sure way to begin and sustain any relationship.

Now when you think of ego, what comes to mind? Does this seem like a difficult way to begin? I remember being a cheerleader and selecting various players to shout out to highlight their plays. They loved hearing us shout and get the crowd going. Take some time and write down three things that you would say is amazing about yourself. Often the good we see in ourselves we attract in others. This is how we complement each other. Taking the time to define the things about yourself is an important way to develop ways of knowing how to spot the light in others by developing your own internal cheerleader.

Highlight is next. Highlight is simply referencing something you heard the person say or do. Some people may call this parroting back. Choose one thing to highlight and say that is amazing, good or something positive. When others speak it is important to show that you are listening to what was said. When others feel seen and heard, trust can be established. It also gives you credit for creating a vulnerable space where you put your current needs and desires aside to make space for someone else. This is a sure way to put a smile on someone's face. I absolutely love making others feel good. Our energy depletes when we don't take time to vibe with others. Finding the right vibration is key to establishing a true connection.

I remember as a student in college using my highlighter to study in my textbooks. I used the highlighter to draw attention to the most salient parts of a text, especially as I thought about future assignments and tests. By highlighting, it helped me to remember key words, dates, or topics. Similarly, meaningful connections are established when we take the time to highlight the important features of others that we have the opportunity to interact with for the first time or as part of an ongoing relationship. Remember, it is key to establish something positive in order to anchor your next steps.

Let me explain further. As a teacher, I would walk around my classroom sharing what I either saw another student doing or highlight something I heard them say. This mid-workshop interruption helped my students feel validated and confident. When I highlighted them, they wanted to do more to get my attention. They knew every day that I was going to highlight someone, and they couldn't wait! I loved watching the smile on their little faces.

Just like egocentric five-year-olds, adults also thrive on compliments. This boost acknowledging a conversation, a scent, an outfit or anything you can find will help to create a space for interest in what could be next or created. A highlight can include simply saying I love, I appreciate, I feel or acknowledge something amazing about someone. If you can't find anything, you probably need to go back to the ego and listen for something that can captivate your interest or attention.

Positive psychology is the study of the conditions and processes that contribute to the flourishing or optimal functioning of people, groups, and institutions (Gable and Haidt, 2005). On a given day, people have about three positive experiences to each negative experience. Taking the time to offer a highlight to someone can change the trajectory of the day. Understanding the importance of highlighting something can offer a true lasting connection. Remember true connection and service leads to a genuine way to build any relationship.

Grenville Kleiser shared that "Good humor is a tonic for mind and body. It is the best antidote for anxiety and depression. It is a business asset. It attracts and keeps friends. It lightens human burdens. It is the direct route to serenity and contentment" (Inspiration and Ideas, 1918).

Humor is my absolute favorite way of connecting with others. Once you have established a clear connection with someone and offered a highlight, the last step is to bring some levity into the space. Sharing a joke or just creating an opportunity to laugh at something is the key. Similarly, I have found that while establishing relationships with others and creating a space for future business, it is important to bring humor into your conversation. Laughing adds value to your physical and mental health and adds social benefits.

First, laughter physically boosts immunity, lowers stress hormones and decreases pain. While making connections with others, offering a chance to relax and to show up authentically is another benefit of humor. Secondly, humor while showing up authentically adds joy and zest to life, eases anxiety and tension, and improves our mood. There is something special about being around someone who just makes you just want to smile and feel good. Lastly, humor strengthens social relationships by attracting others to us, enhancing teamwork and promotes bonding. When used as a tool, humor offers a meaningful way to sustain any relationship and to keep others coming back for more. When you have the audacity to speak, it is critical to show up with humor in order to offer opportunities to engage without fear.

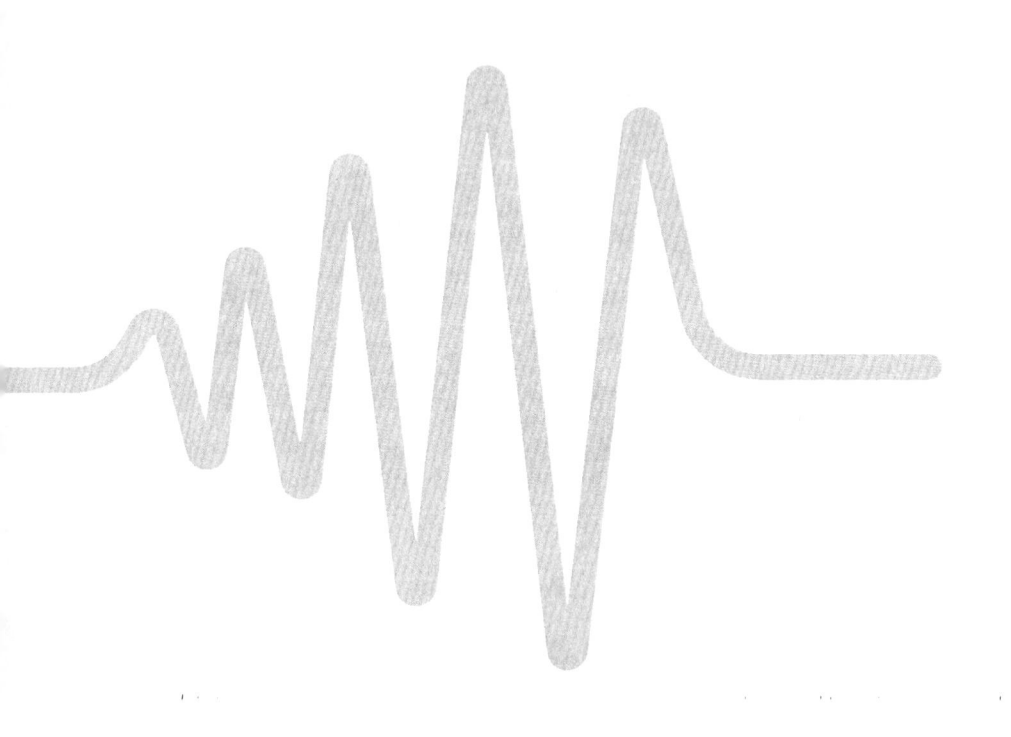

CHAPTER 7

Conclusion

The audacity to speak is simply having the courage to connect. Thus, this book was anchored in the idea that each of us has the capacity to speak; sometimes, we just need the courage to do so. Every opportunity that we have to interact with others can either stretch or shrink us. Understanding that every interaction we have with others can propel us to even greater opportunities can cause us to expand our opportunities and capabilities for making a greater impact in the lives of others.

There are three fundamental ingredients to every conversation that will help you to have a lasting, meaningful and memorable interaction. Relationships have the capacity to hurt or help us to reach our potential.

Every day, we have an opportunity to be better, by actions, thoughts and words. Don't allow the things you have been freed of keep you hostage and/or stuck in your past. New life, opportunities and cultivated relationships can benefit the entire universe. Paying particular attention to our words energizes us to want to achieve.

Our intention with our words has the power to transform. This change can impact lives, generations, and situations. To start, take the time to assess your current situation and select the words that are aligned to your authentic self and the outcomes that you see for yourself. If you do take the time to speak up, you will be proud of yourself and cultivate your inner voice. Take control of your future and speak life into your situation. Allow others the opportunity to behave as they will but knowing you have had your say. Remember when the purpose of a thing is not clear, abuse is inevitable. Don't give anyone a license to mistreat you because of your lack of courage. The core of our being is the ultimate reality, and no one can take this power from you. You determine the results because your ultimate power comes from within.

The moment when you get it, you have to face, deal with, accept or go through it, its time. It is time to accept this challenge that you are about to go through; it is ordained, sanctioned and necessary to give yourself permission to grow and to live authentically. And if you don't believe me, that's fine; keep living. Every photo gets exposed and sees the light of day.

Audacity To Speak

I've learned a long time ago that the same things you try to avoid come back anyway, so you might at least go through it. These are things that you try to avoid and end up coming right back around for you to face. So I accept my fate, I will do my assignment. It does just make you want to holla.

To facilitate this process, I recommend that you make a list of things that you have to do, and what would happen if you do not do them—this is both the what and the why? Then what. What would happen if you don't say what it is that you wanted to say?

I am clear that I have been brought to a place of understanding that I can see, hear and sense the people around me and that I am committed to being obedient to God.

As we close out our journey together, I want to remind you that how we choose to interact with others matters. It matters because we have the ability to lift someone into new opportunities, and it starts with our words. There is something to offer everyone who we come in contact with. The lasting impact that we leave others helps to plant seeds of relationships. The following are just a few words of affirmations that can propel you forward as you gain the audacity to speak.

- I love the life I have while I create the life of my dreams.
- I believe in my potential not my past.
- Everything is right about you, and it is such a gift to be able to be around you.

As you reflect about the insight and offerings of Audacity to Speak, I want to first thank you for this opportunity to journey into the unknown with me. It is my hope that you will apply new knowledge, skills, and information that you learned in this book during challenging times and when dealing with others (family, coworkers, community members) who are stuck in old patterns. Most importantly, it is my sincerest hope that you will embrace the power within you, unmute, and speak.

Works Consulted

Brené Brown. *Daring Greatly*. Penguin Random House: New York, 2012.

Gable, Shelly L. and Haidt, Jonathan. *What (and Why) is Positive Psychology?* First Published June 1, 2005; Vol 9, Issue 2, 2005

Glaser Judith. *Conversational Intelligence*. Bibliomotion: Brookline, MA, 2013.

Kleiser, Greenville. *Inspiration and Ideas*. Funk & Wagnalls: New York, 1918.

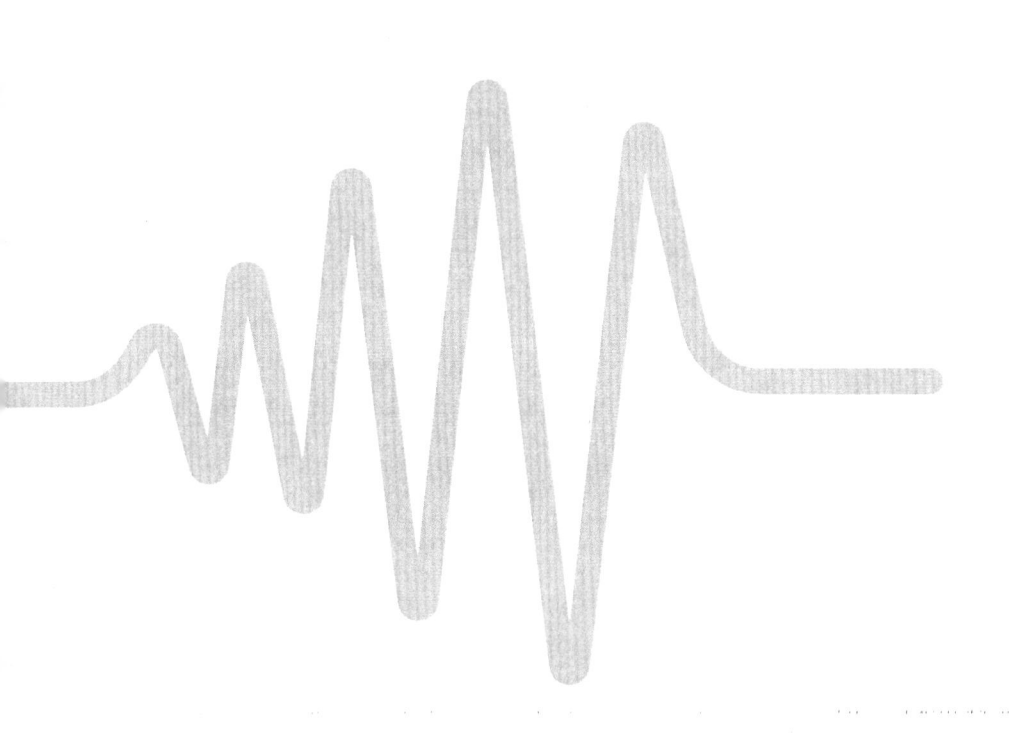

APPENDIX

- 74 -

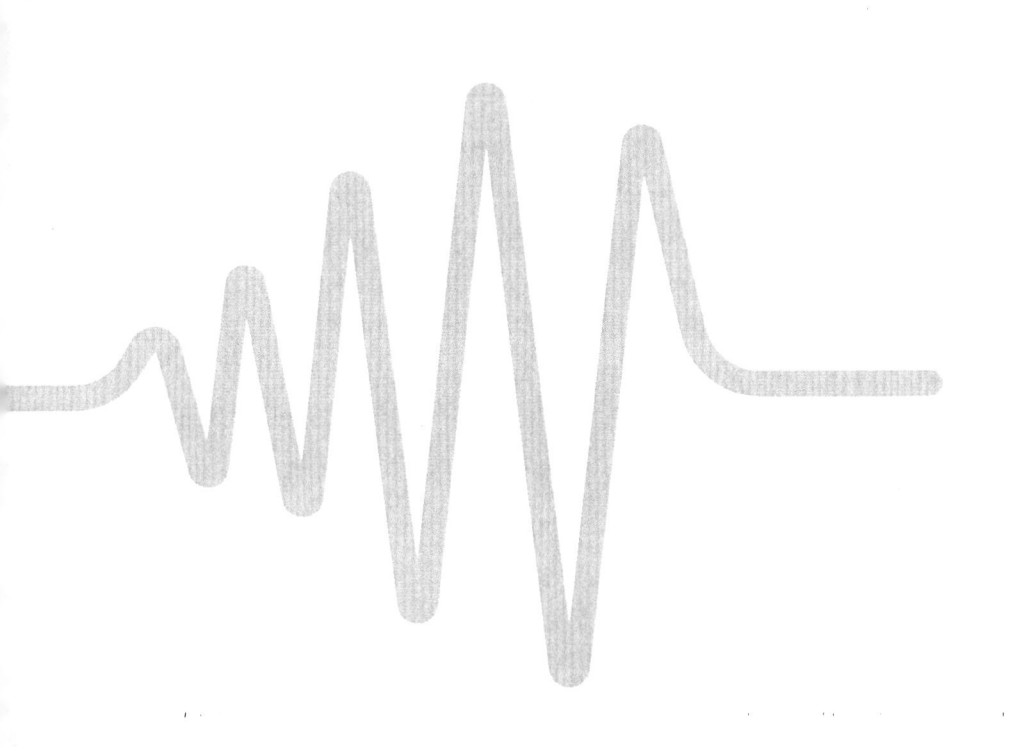

THE BIOCODE SYSTEM™
EMPOWERMENT WORKOUT

FOR LEADERS

IMAGINE...

Being so empowered that you can get through
a single day without anyone driving you crazy

Having the resilience and strength to
navigate challenging situations

When life comes at you, instead of needing to
take the day off,
you're going to be ready to

TAKE THE DAY ON

THE BIOCODE SYSTEM™

BioCode 1:
Insider Codes | Self-Empowerment

BioCode 2:
Workout Codes | Inner Strength

BioCode 3:
Timing Codes | Self-Regulation

BioCode 4:
Talk Codes | Effortless Communication

BioCode 5:
Walk Codes | Self-Navigation

"Life is in your favor... if you know how to take it on!"

RULES TO THE GAME

WHO ARE THE PLAYERS? YOU.
It's all about you. This is solo work.

Tip: No one has to change other than you. Most work is done anonymously through this process of learning.

WHERE IS THIS GYM? YOUR EVERYDAY LIFE.
Your work, family, friends and responsibilities are your gym.

Tip: This is a problem-solving world. Your lessons appear through daily conflict, the good, bad and ugly.

WHAT ARE THE WEIGHTS? STRESSORS. (INTERNAL & EXTERNAL)
Your "weights of life," are the situations that cause you to weaken and are here to strengthen you.

Tip: When life pushes against you, it shows you what lives within yourself. View problems, stress and pain as instruments for growth.

WHEN DO I PRACTICE? ANYTIME A CHALLENGE ARISES
The exercises are performed when something feels uncomfortable.

Tip: It's always your turn. Even if pain is triggered from other people's weakness or behaviors, it's still your opportunity to grow.

CATCH YOUR WEAKNESS

BEFORE	DURING	AFTER

|—————— AWARENESS SCALE ——————|

- There are 3 opportunities to "CATCH YOUR WEAKNESS" while dealing with challenges.

- Your ability to stay functional during difficult situations will fluctuate.

- Your levels of awareness to change depend on the difficulty of the situation.

- Remember there is no right or wrong, only opportunities to grow.

- You get unlimited do-overs.

- You couldn't do this work wrong even if you tried.

WORK YOUR MOMENTS

A NEW WAY OF THINKING

BUILDS HABITS TO PRODUCE
INNER STRENGTH
WHOLE-LIFE TRANSFORMATION

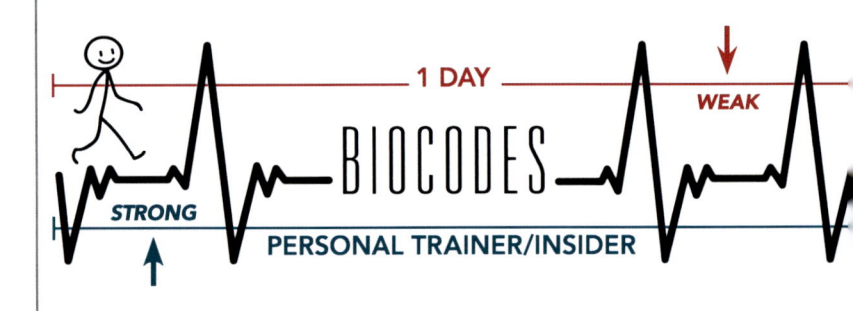

———— 1 DAY ————
WEAK
BIOCODES
STRONG
PERSONAL TRAINER/INSIDER

- ✓ PLAY YOUR WEAKNESS
- ✓ SET YOUR GOALS LOW
- ✓ MEASURED BY FLUCTUATING GROWTH
- ✓ INNER DIRECTED
- ✓ GROW WITH PRAISE
- ✓ HIGHLY INDEPENDENT

"Empowerment begins at the intersection of your thoughts and habits."

BioCode 1: Insider Codes

SELF-EMPOWERMENT

GOAL
To train your focus to see all problems as instruments for personal growth. As you strengthen, you will empower others naturally.

NEW PERSPECTIVE
It's all about you. You are responsible for your life. You are powerless to change anyone other than yourself. This is solo work.

"Stay functional and let life adjust to you."

SELF-EMPOWERMENT

BioCode 1: Insider Codes

STEP 1. AWARENESS
Identify your focal point.

When you're in a challenging situation, check in, observe where your focus is – on you or on someone else?

STEP 2. ADJUST
Bring your focus back to yourself.

Regardless of who is right or wrong, keep your focus on your conduct only.

STEP 3. ACTION
Practice staying in your power regardless of the difficulty of the circumstance.

Practicing this discipline turns all challenges into opportunities to become a stronger leader.

"Where your mind goes your life grows."

BioCode 1: Insider Codes

SELF-EMPOWERMENT: Metaphor

HOLD ON IN THE STORM

WHAT KEEPS YOU STUCK

- Thinking the solution is outside of yourself.
- Getting caught in the winds of the problem.

"The stronger you become the stronger you are for others."

SELF-EMPOWERMENT: Check in

BioCode 1: Insider Codes

KEEP THE FOCUS ON YOU

Check in: During the stormy situations, am I in control or am I swept into the storm?

Check in: Do I think the solution comes from inner direction or outer correction?

Check in: Whose behavior am I focused on – mine or someone else's?

Check in: Who is the person complaining – me or the other person?

Check in: Am I crossing the fence without permission or am I staying on my side?

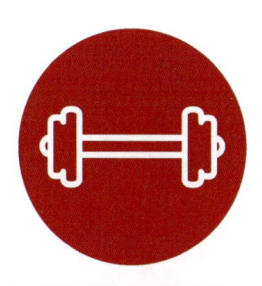

BioCode 2: Workout Codes

INNER STRENGTH

GOAL
To practice your inner-workout daily to build your weaker emotional muscles.

NEW PERSPECTIVE
Your emotional weaknesses are strengths in disguise when exercised properly.

"Your life is your gym, get stronger in it."

INNER STRENGTH

BioCode 2: Workout Codes

STEP 1. AWARENESS
Go fishing for weaker thoughts. Catch your story and label it with a **one word** emotion to describe how it makes you feel.

Example: I feel frustrated, worried, doubtful.

STEP 2. ADJUST
Find the exact opposite word. Pain is your indicator showing you the weak muscle that needs strengthening.

Example: Frustration/Patience, Worry/Trust, Doubt/Confidence

STEP 3. ACTION
Practice saying the opposite word in that moment. Like exercising a weak muscle, it takes repetition and must be done regardless of how you feel or function to get stronger.

Example: Say "Practice patience," "Practice trust," "Practice confidence."

"Your power comes from working the moment, not just living in it."

BioCode 2: Workout Codes

INNER STRENGTH: New Model

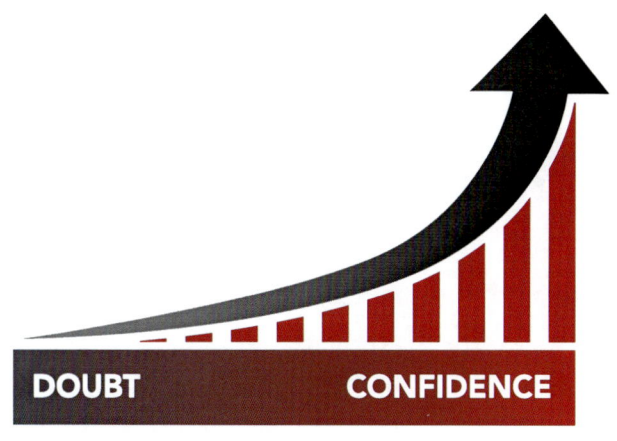

DOUBT — **CONFIDENCE**

ONE EMOTIONAL SYSTEM

WHAT KEEPS YOU STUCK

- Dwelling on your weaker emotional words.
- Categorizing emotions as negative or positive.

INNER STRENGTH: Opposite Chart

BioCode 2: Workout Codes

SAME EMOTION (DUAL WORDS)

FEEL THIS WEAKER WORDS	PRACTICE THIS STRONGER WORDS
Fear	Safety
Doubt	Confidence
Overwhelm	Calm
Judgement	Acceptance
Guilt	Innocence
Worry	Trust
Insecurity	Security
Frustration	Patience
Expectation	Observation

Example: Doubt = Weakness in Confidence

BioCode 3: Timing Codes

SELF-REGULATION

GOAL
To observe when emotions are elevated to know if it is most beneficial to talk, walk or listen.

NEW PERSPECTIVE
The only functional time to interact and problem solve are when all parties are emotionally neutral.

"Walk before you talk, think before you speak."

SELF-REGULATION

BioCode 3: Timing Codes

STEP 1. AWARENESS
Observe if you are in an unstable or stormy situation.

STEP 2. ADJUST
Pause. Where is the storm coming from—you, someone else or both.

STEP 3. ACTION
You: If your emotions are elevated, calmly move away from others or refrain from speaking to stabilize yourself before interacting.

Others: If someone else's emotions are elevated, kindly redirect yourself away from them or listen supportively without trying to solve the problem.

Practice impulse control by delaying your direct interactions until everyone's emotions are neutral.

"Observe everything, expect nothing."

SELF-REGULATION: Metaphor

BioCode 3: Timing Codes

HIT THE PAUSE BUTTON

WHAT KEEPS YOU STUCK

- Feeding the fire. Trying to problem solve when emotions are elevated.
- Not noticing you just got emotionally hijacked.

"It's more important to be kind than to be right."

SELF-REGULATION: Chart

BioCode 3: Timing Codes

EMOTIONAL STATES

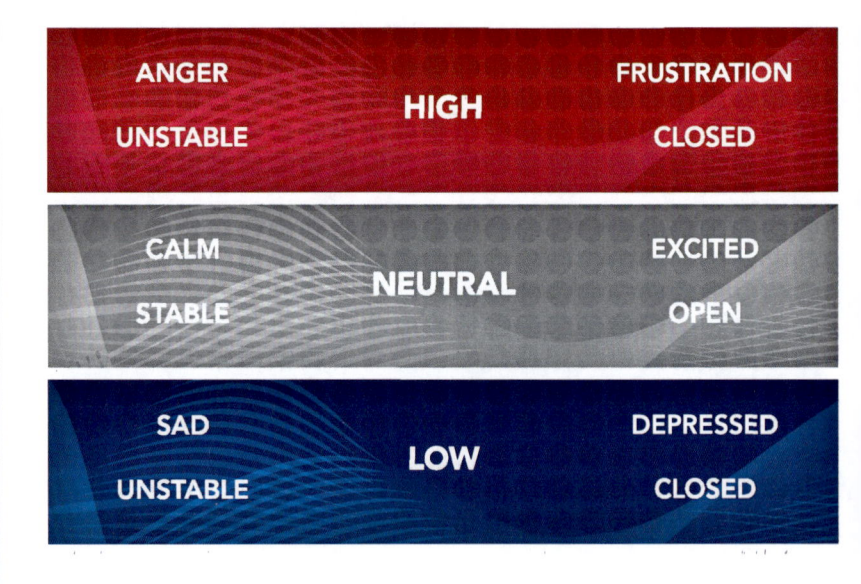

ANGER	**HIGH**	FRUSTRATION
UNSTABLE		CLOSED

CALM	**NEUTRAL**	EXCITED
STABLE		OPEN

SAD	**LOW**	DEPRESSED
UNSTABLE		CLOSED

"When emotions run high, words lie."

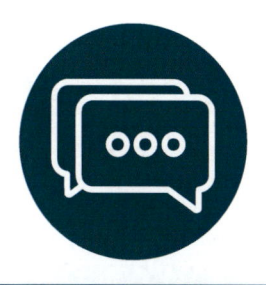

BioCode 4: Talk Codes

EFFORTLESS COMMUNICATION

GOAL
To express yourself effectively, regardless of the weaker words or actions of others.

NEW PERSPECTIVE
There are hidden good intentions that can be found behind dysfunctional words. You can create healthy interactions regardless of how things are said.

"Make the next right move regardless of how things are said or done."

EFFORTLESS COMMUNICATION

BioCode 4: Talk Codes

STEP 1. AWARENESS
Recognize when a conversation is challenging.

Tip: Assume the other person is trying to ask for what they need, not just complaining.

STEP 2. ADJUST
Find the underlying good intention. Silently translate the weaker words into: "I want...I'd like... or I'd prefer."

STEP 3. ACTION
Respond to your translated words as if they said it that way originally.

Practice putting the message back out in better words than it came in.

"Don't make anyone wrong or take anything personally, except the good."

EFFORTLESS COMMUNICATION

BioCode 4: Talk Codes

SAMPLE SCRIPT

They say (Weaker words): "You didn't do it right."

What they are really trying to say: "I'd prefer things to be done differently. "

Your Response (Stronger Words): "Let's look together to see what we can do to improve this."

Tip: This will dramatically help reduce conflict and keep conversations productive.

EFFORTLESS COMMUNICATION

BioCode 4: Talk Codes

SPIN STRAW   TO GOLD

PUT WORDS OUT BETTER THAN THEY CAME IN

WHAT KEEPS YOU STUCK

- Taking things personally. Believing words or actions are meant to hurt.
- Thinking they should know how to say things right.

BioCode 5: Walk Codes

SELF-NAVIGATION

GOAL
To keep your focus forward by being fluid, flexible and changing quickly when things are not going according to plan.

NEW PERSPECTIVE
Life is always here to help guide you. If you don't make the changes needed, life will do it for you.

"Fall in love with the unknown...that's where your gifts are."

SELF-NAVIGATION

BioCode 5: Walk Codes

STEP 1. AWARENESS
Observe if you are in a "stuck situation."

Tip: Whenever you feel trapped, rejected or excluded, stop and notice the door is closed.

STEP 2. ADJUST
Consider other choices to help you move forward.

Tip: Trust the new direction will ultimately lead you to a better outcome than you can see today.

STEP 3. ACTION
Practice redirecting away from things that don't serve you without taking anything personally or making anyone wrong.

Tip: People that are flexible and not attached to specific outcomes will move faster and create new possibilities effortlessly.

"Do the next right thing anyway."

SELF-NAVIGATION: Metaphor

**THERE IS NO REJECTION
ONLY DIRECTION AND REDIRECTION**

WHAT KEEPS YOU STUCK

- Blame and victim mentality. Woulda… Coulda… Shoulda… If… Then… When… Then…
- Feeling rejected by the change, questioning why this happened.

"Always redirect kindly away from things that don't serve you."

BioCode 5: Walk Codes

SELF-NAVIGATION: Graphic

BioCode 5: Walk Codes

FOCUS HERE

MICRO MOVES=MACRO CHANGE

1. Set your intention
2. Drop all expectations to outcomes
3. Become fluid and flexible along the way
4. Your gifts are coming from unexpected places and surprises

"Small change over time creates huge change in time."

GUIDING PRINCIPLES

BE YOU
Take responsibility for your leadership/life.

BE PURPOSEFUL
Trust that you are born to succeed.

BE EMPOWERED
Work your moments. That is where inner strength is built.

BE RESILIENT
Allow yourself to make mistakes to learn better for the next time.

BE AUTHENTIC
Stay congruent with your words, interactions and advice.

BE NICE
Lead with kindness. You only grow through praise, not criticism.

BE EXCITED
Fall in love with the unknown, that's where your gifts are.

BE O.K.
Relax, you have BioCodes to help guide you.

EMPOWERHOUSE
LEADERSHIP CONSULTANCY

www.empowerhousegroup.com
empowerhousegroup@gmail.com

Made in United States
North Haven, CT
10 November 2022